The Spooks

Michaela Morgan

Illustrated by Daniel Postgate

OXFORD
UNIVERSITY PRESS

1

Meet the Spooks

Would you like to meet
the Spooks?

Well, come on in.

Here they are.
They are:

Mr and Mrs Spook

Mum and Dad Spook,

Luke the
Spook,

Luke

Moaning
Lisa
and
Baby Boo.

BOO!

This is their pet bat, Tibbles.

They all lived together in Tottering Towers.

Tottering Towers was an old, old house.
The Spooks had lived here for hundreds
of years.

The garden was untidy, the pond
was smelly and the house was dusty,
musty, messy and tumbling down.

But the Spooks loved it.

Some of the people who lived in the town *didn't* love it.

They said, 'This place needs tidying up. No one will want to visit our town if it looks a mess!'

The Spooks loved the house just as it was. They didn't want *anything* to change.

One day, another family
moved into Tottering Towers.

The Spooks stared at the new family.

'It's the Normal family,' groaned
Mum and Dad Spook. 'Their
grandparents used to live here. So did
their great-grandparents and their
great-great-great-grandparents…'

'No parents are *that* great,' moaned
Lisa.

This was the Normal family:
Mum, the twins Norman and
Norma, the baby, Babette
and their pet cat, Nigel.
'They all look as normal
as normal can be!' said
Luke the Spook.

'Oh, wow!' said Norman and
Norma, when they saw the house.
'I'm not sure it's safe…' Mum
worried. A bit of wall had fallen down
and there were cracks everywhere.

'Don't worry, Mum,' said Norman.
'We can fix it up bit by bit,' added
Norma. 'Bit by bit! Bit by bit!' sang
Baby Babette.

'There are some spooks here, of
course,' Mum added, 'but they're
harmless.'

'That's what *they* think!' hissed Luke
the Spook.

2

Nightmare Neighbours!

Both the Normal Family and the Spooks
liked to do the same sort of things.
Both families liked to make a lot of noise.

Both Norma Normal and Moaning Lisa liked to moan.

The two pets both liked to hunt.

There was one big difference.

The Normal family were awake and noisy all day.

The Spook family were awake and noisy *all night*.

By the end of the first week, both families had exactly the same idea.

They've got to go!

3

Tricks, Tricks and More Tricks

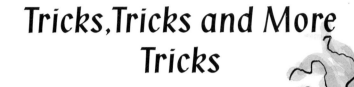

'Girls and boys make too much noise!' said the Spooks.

'Those ghosts are toast!' said the Normals.

That bat is nasty and catty.

That cat is silly and batty.

So the battle began.

The two families played tricks on each other.
There were tricks, tricks and more tricks.
There was a lot of taunting and teasing.

Things went
EEK!
in the night.

As the two families battled, the house wobbled and shook.

Dust rose, cobwebs fell, cracks grew wider and wider until...

... **KERRUMP!**

The chimney fell down.

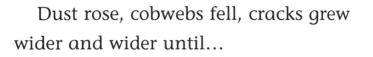

4

Don't knock our house down!

The firemen arrived, the police arrived and the mayor and a crowd of grumpy people arrived.

'This house is not safe,' they said to the Normals. 'If you can't fix it up, you will have to move out.'

'Yay! Yaaaaaaa!' cheered the Spooks.

A few of the firemen looked nervous.

The mayor looked worried but he said, 'We will knock this house down. That will be *much* safer! Then we can build a very useful supermarket here, or some offices… or maybe a motorway.'

'Nooo!' moaned the Spooks. 'Don't knock our home down! Oh, noooooo!'

NOOOO!

NOOOO!

When they heard all this howling,
the firemen looked very nervous. The
police looked worried. The mayor and
all the grumpy people looked terrified!

NOOOO! NOOOO! NOOOO!

'What's *that*?' they all cried.

Oh, that's just the Spooks,' said
Norma. 'They can be pests!'

'Noooooo! Not true!' howled the
Spooks.

The people looked
interested.

The firemen looked *very*
interested and the
mayor looked
excited...

'Aha!' he said. 'Oh, ho!' he said.
'Spooks, eh?'

He went off to mutter
to the group of grumpy
people.

Then the
mayor came
back.

'We've made up our minds!' he said.
'A haunted house is just what we need
in this town!'

'And you can charge money for
tickets,' he added.

'You can use the money to fix the
place up,' said a helpful policeman.

The Normals and the Spooks had a
meeting.

'If we want to stay here, we're going
to have to work together,' they said.

So that's what they did.

They made posters. They made tickets.

They were in the newspapers. They even went on television.

Then the visitors started to arrive – and so did the money.

JULY

MON.	TUES.	WED.	THURS.	FRI.	SAT.	SUN.
SPOOKS	NORMALS	SPOOKS	NORMALS	SPOOKS	NORMALS	

The two families worked out a timetable.

On Mondays, Wednesdays and Fridays the Spooks did their tricks.

They whooped and they swooped. They clinked and they clanked. They appeared and they disappeared – and the baby shouted **Boo!**

They were quite tired on the other days… so they could sleep.

On Tuesdays, Thursdays and Saturdays, the Normal family got busy with the building work. This meant that on the other days they were so tired they could sleep through anything.

On Sundays both families had a rest.

So that's how two very different families learned to get on with each other.

They became the best of friends.

'We're different,' said Luke.

'But we're different in the same sort of way!' said Norman.

Did they live happily ever after?

Well, they *almost* did but… the cat and the bat never, ever really learned to love each other.

About the author

I have written more than
100 books for children. I
usually start by
daydreaming, and then
I move on to scribbling the
story down. I type it on my
computer, and then I check it,
re-work it and re-work it again
until I think it is right.

I think very hard about the pictures too.
I imagine each page in my head.
I like spooky stories and I like funny stories.
I hope you do, too!